THERE IS NO UNIVERSE

RUSS SIMMONS

There Is No Universe

Copyright © 2021 by *Russ Simmons*

All rights reserved. No part of this publication may be reproduced, distributed, or transmitted in any form or by any means, including photocopying, recording, or other electronic or mechanical methods, without the prior written permission of the author, except in the case of brief quotations embodied in critical reviews and certain other non-commercial uses permitted by copyright law.

ISBN
978-1-954932-40-1 (Paperback)
978-1-954932-39-5 (eBook)

PREFACE

The Universe is a "state of mind",
…… God's mind.

There is no physical Universe, only
the perception of an endless expanse.

There Is No Universe

Revelation 4:5
*-From the throne came flashes of lightning, rumblings and peals of thunder. In front of the throne, **seven** lamps were blazing. These are the **seven spirits** of **God**.*
The author here speaks for the "seven spirits of the Lord." We reside in one of these houses, or
level, of God's spirit. This physical presence of earth is a level of God's spirit. Our reason for being here is to improve our spirit in order to reach the next higher level of God's universe.

John 14:2
*-My Father's house has **many rooms**; if that were not so, would I have told you that I am going there to prepare a place for you?*
This is the seven levels of Gods mind, with many being in this physical plane, or universe, and one being the ultimate goal of all-knowing Heaven. God gives us this physical map of planets and galaxies so we have a location and for expansion of our physical minds. Scientist tell us the universe is "expanding." This plane is the thought of God, always moving, always fluid. It must seem to expand to keep ahead of the human

education. With each lifetime we have the free will to elevate our soul or likewise decrease our soul's level. This is totally each person's responsibility and achievement.

James, 4:14
-Why, you do not even know what will happen tomorrow. What is your life? You are a mist that appears for a little while and then vanishes.
This is the closest to a correct description of our existence. A mist, a dream, a God thought; all powerful and all encompassing, but still just that: a mist. A very important mist for our own development of being. If we are only aware of the physical world around us, we are not accomplishing God's purpose for us. We are here at this place and time to elevate our souls to the Christ conscience level.

This book is not written to change your mind on any beliefs or religion. It's one and only purpose is to make you THINK and question. Think about anything that anyone, and I mean anyone, tells you about how you should believe on any subject. Thinking is most important for your religious beliefs and your eternal soul. Think about and consider the words and ideas in this book.

TABLE OF CONTENTS

TRUTH ONE – prayer – why pray – prayer vs. meditation – Christian meditation

TRUTH TWO – the universe – plane of existence – levels of Gods existence

TRUTH THREE – God is logic – previous lives

TRUTH FOUR – what is religion? – study to develop

TRUTH FIVE – religions and prayer – different types of expression

TRUTH SIX – know God

TRUTH SEVEN - second coming of Christ – human understanding of =The Word

TRUTH ONE

There Is No Universe

Scientist use the phrase "the expanding universe". How is that possible? We all have contemplated this concept but give up feeling it is just beyond our limited understanding. There is always a logical explanation to everything. The only reason the universe is "expanding" is because our earthly physical technology is improving to explore visually into the perception called universe. God's mind existence can expand the universe to stay ahead of our own physical development. We are here, we truly exist, but here is not all there is. This plane of being is a "state of mind", Gods mind. The Bible writes of the "seven spirits (houses) of the Lord." This means the seven levels of Gods mind. Several levels are in this physical plane and one being the ultimate Heaven. Are there six, five, four, etc. levels here, not sure. Are other levels on other planets in this universe, not sure. There is no universe, only the perception of an endless expanse so as to locate us in this physical existence. In James, chapter four, this mist is the universe. This is the closest to a correct description of our existence that can be found in the Bible. We, being in this plane, can only see and experience what is around us that the developing technology will allow but our real existence here is to elevate our souls to the Christ level so we can know more of what is really out there for us.

Consider this:

(James 3:9)
With the tongue we praise our Lord and Father, and with it we curse human beings, who have been made in God's likeness.

What a bold statement. But, it is in the Bible therefore we must consider it a valid point. Religions have been reading and saying this for thousands of years but never give it a serious thought. "God's likeness", Does that mean God has two arm and five fingers? I very much doubt it. The likeness is in the soul, the spirit. We have this likeness to God so we can communicate directly with Him. Any level spirit can talk to and listen to God's thoughts so as to evolve to be more righteous in our existence.

Are there other beings on other planets somewhere out in this "universe"? We as the average person do not know. Maybe others on this planet do know but are withholding that information. But, I cannot believe a God of such magnitude could not minister to more than just one small planet of humans. This plane of existence can surely support more than one planet of beings. Think "out of the box." Is it logical to believe that God would create an endless physical level of universe and have only one planet of beings? There is no universe that is all to end all physical space. We are here in our little place of being but this is not the only plane or level. Remember, there are seven levels of universe (God's spirit) and we are but a small part in this grand scheme. Is planet Earth God's level THREE and planet Krypton (just to have a name) is God's level 5? No one knows but I believe this concept is worth considering. Maybe your next lifetime will not be on this planet Earth.

In God's highest level "Heaven" there is no race or gender. This would explain why most physical visits by spirits are images and not clear visions? A spirit is not a ghost. The ghosts we hear so much about are troubled individual's souls that are not ready to release and proceed to the next plateau. Keeping in mind the next level for any one individual may not be a higher level. It would seem logical that some are destine to proceed to a lower level of being after a particularly troublesome lifetime. They still have much to learn before proceeding.

Spirits will appear to us in a form that we can understand. They will always appear to us in a format that would resemble a human form. This form is not the true spirit shape only a resemblance of an earthly being. Humans try to keep things simple, like thinking that our present forms will stay with us for eternity. How silly would that be? Work to improve your spiritual self, this is the you forever.

Nothing is simple. Be careful, if you think you know something, other than God is, you probably don't. And yes, there is a God. God is Nature, God Is. Is He anything like we envision? No, and thank God for that. If He was like we thought then He could not have given us this wonderful existence, or what is commonly known as the universe. Is there more than one universe? I would think so. Why not? Can a human soul evolve from one universe to another? I would think that is possible also. Can a spirit make that jump, back and forth if needed? Sure. As the Bible teaches "the seven layers of Heaven" in the universe are we number one or number four level of God's mind. Not sure, but I am convinced it's not number seven, …. Heaven.

TRUTH TWO

God is logic. It would be impossible for God to have an illogical thought, event or outcome. Everything; and I mean everything in God's universe is logical. God is nature. Therefore, everything in nature is logical. In nature, illogical does not exist. Every living and inanimate object is supposed to be here, including us humans. The human mind is the only natural process that has free will and it is under our control so we have the ability to think illogical and do many illogical actions.

If someone (teacher, mentor, preacher, rabbi, priest, etc.) presents a principle or theory to you and claims it to be the "truth" your first reaction should be to think, "Is this logical?" Do not assume they are correct or even that your first thoughts are right. Just because that person has studied a topic and has years in research or education, necessarily means their conclusions are the correct answer. Most humans are led to a belief by other humans. Few ideas are thought about and determined to make up a person's own beliefs. We must think, pray and meditate to reach our own conclusions about any theory and create our own principles and spiritual values. This approach will develop our souls and spirits correctly if done in God's presence. Jesus and others have taught us God's goodness is all around and will never fail us. This God presence must be used it to elevate our souls to higher levels and closer to God's inspiration. Do not follow other humans blindly only to remain on this existing level. The opposite is true also. If we think in our human (illogical) side, evil may prevail. Think only in the God presence and teachings then surely goodness and mercy will prevail for you.

Some will argue that we as lowly humans could not possibly understand Gods logic. The Bible teaches that God will never present to us more than we can handle. We live in and around this all logical nature (God) so just look around, study, think and learn. Man is placed in this physical plane to advance and be able to accept more and more of the understanding of God's mind and plan. Doing and accepting "man" teachings generation after generation is a disservice to God's wishes for us. Nowhere is it written that all humans are at the same level of God understanding. This understanding can and should be personally increasing on a continual basis. Release physical thoughts and limitations and advance to God's unlimited resources. Think God thoughts and God's logic will increase in you.

Now let's think about logic. A child is born with a negative life altering disease or physical condition. What is Gods logic to this? Another child is born with a gift of superior intelligence or talent. What is Gods logic to this? The Bible teaches us that we will suffer for our sins. The case of a newborn infant, where is his/

her sin for a life of discomfort? Remember, everything in nature (God) is logical. The only logical explanation is sin from a previous life. Physical life is a teaching/learning experience. God uses each lifetime to give us the opportunity to improve our spiritual selves. Many think we live this life then die and wait in heaven for Jesus return. This is very illogical and elementary. This also goes against all Biblical teachings. God created this physical nature to be self-sustaining and self-perpetuating. Where is the evolution of our souls if we depend on this short stay on earth then spend the rest of eternity in Heaven? This idea would seem to be totally illogical. If this were the total of life there is not much incentive for good and worthy progression. We as humans are a part of this nature, both living this physical life and living the spiritual life.

Physical nature is constantly evolving so we humans are to evolve likewise in both planes physical and spiritual.

Organized religion persons think that if we knew we had other lives then we would do wrong (sin) because we would be lazy, believing there is time later to repent. I disagree. If any individual knows any sin will be accounted for and in a future life then the desire to improve and do good is encouraged. This pay it forward attitude incentive program will give us a better, more satisfying life in this and future lives.

Don't misunderstand; we as a society need religious leaders and teachers. Humans are purposely intended to be social creatures. We need groups of others to discuss ideas then learn from thoughts or opinions of others. On this plane of existence are many levels of spiritual maturity. So, it is the responsibility of teachers and/or parents to help advance their students or children to higher levels. Not to keep teaching the same dialog, same stories without dwelling deeper for more meaning generation after generation. This dis-service is holding the audience to the same level of spiritual growth through an entire lifetime. Religious leaders must advance their spirits so as to advance the pupil's. And as students of God we must listen, think, meditate with God then, and only then, form our own opinion and beliefs. Doing this will get us closer to God and elevate our souls to higher meanings.

Trial, yes lots of trial and tribulation in this physical life and all lives in the future. Think of each life as a constant school, day and night, seven days a week. (James 1:12), *Blessed is the one (man/woman) who perseveres under trial, because* **when** *he has stood the test, he* **will** *receive the crown of life that God has promised to those who love Him.* If you read further from here "Him" is God. This will be true whether you are physically rich or poor. All humans will be tested and God will grade us on how we accept the problems and how we solve them. Yes, just like when we were children in school. Life is a constant school. Can you go through the trials presented and maintain or increase your faith and love of God? He has made this an open book test with The Bible and other religious books. Problem is many persons use these writings to justify and advance human desires. Some study the Bible out of a since of duty without thinking about the true meanings. *Studying any religious book literally* is wrong and non-productive to a higher purpose. God also gives us the knowledge that if we ask, and know, He will resolve our issues for us. Key word here is KNOW.

Here's something to think about. In Matthew 9: 1-8 Jesus heals a paralytic. Jesus says *Take heart, son; your sins are forgiven*. Why does Jesus associate a physical ailment with sins? Later in this story Jesus proclaims that he has the "authority on earth to forgive sins." Is this lesson to inform us that all physical and mental illnesses are to be linked to sin? It would sure seem so. This is a very scary theory that a lot of people will want to disagree with or ignore. But, Jesus confirms this idea in several lessons of the Bible. What better of an incentive to strive for a sin free lifetime in this life and all future lives than to realize that God has established a system of fairness and accountability for our own actions. This concept is logical because multiple lives are necessary to develop maturity and deeper soul searching.

We as students of the Bible, and believers of the Bible teachings must accept all of the teachings, especially the newer, more advanced concepts that Jesus brought to us. The problem is that too many people do not want to think. As I have been saying, we as the children of God must use the information that Jesus left to elevate our souls. He told us how it really is but the truth is uncomfortable. People tend to twist the lessons in the Bible to make themselves, or others feel better or to explain a situation at hand in a way that is easy to understand even if it may not be the real issue.

TRUTH THREE

Do not pray for things you want or for events you want to happen. The Bible has already told you that God knows what your needs and desires are.

(Philippians 4:19)
And my God will meet all your needs according to the riches of his glory in Christ Jesus.

This sounds strange because you have been taught this method of prayer since childhood. We are all guilty of this and in our hearts know it's not the most desired way that Christ would have us worship. So why pray? We pray to become more Christ like. To mature in this physical plane, so all needs will come to you to make your life more pleasurable and freer of need. Thank God for what he will do for you in the future and be appreciative of what God just did for you in the past. Wisdom, a word used frequently in the Bible.

(James 1:5)
If any of you lacks wisdom, you should ask God, who gives generously to all without finding fault, and it will be given to you. But, continues on to warn us: *But when you ask, you must believe and not doubt, because the one who doubts is like a wave of the sea, blown and tossed by the wind.*

(James 1:6) In other words, we must <u>know</u> that God is going to grant our wish. If you have any doubt your request it will not be received from God. Bad people receive a lot of things they should not. And you know they did not receive it by asking God. Earthly possessions can be received through earthly activities. But, these will be shortly retained and will not assist at all to elevate your spiritual self and may even harm the spirit.

Do you need 10 million dollars in the bank? Well, none of us would mind but that may not be want you need to develop in this life time; maybe next time. God will bless you as needed and because of your blessings to Him. Nature will always meet your needs. That is a direct promise. Only God can and will determine what blessings are the best for you and for your development. Just because a person prays for the 10 million dollars, we all know God does not mean automatic receipt in a short period of time. Maybe He has other ways to grant you 10 million dollars of value. Or maybe He is waiting for you to be ready and secure before granting any prayer request. The answer could be in a totally other future lifetime.

The Bible teaches us everything we need to know

to be more "<u>Christ like.</u>" But our human, "free will", minds allow us to pick out certain passages and apply them where and when we want. We tend to leave out lessons or ideas that do not serve our desired goal. You cannot do this. If you profess to believe the Bible and Jesus' teachings you must profess to all of it. Now the Bible is written in a human understanding form and we all know we must think about what the message is, not the details of the story. Study, think, pray, meditate over the teacher's words. These are the lessons that will benefit us most. Jesus' whole reason for existence was to educate the future generations on how to mature and elevate our souls in this existence, in this universal plane designed by God.

How should one pray? First, let's make a distinction between prayer and meditation. And yes, there is a difference. Many people believe meditation is wrong, almost sinful. To them it brings up ideas of old fashion devil worship and "God fearing" Christians are not to practice it. Nothing could be further from the truth. Anything can be done incorrectly and most people do not know how to meditate correctly because they have never been taught. Prayer is an important event in our human experience. One, it does as Christ taught, witness' to the world our belief in a supreme God and two is a method to be humble and giving thanks to God's blessings. Prayer is done in Church, before or after a sporting event or anytime in a group of others. Also, while driving, flying, or riding in any vehicle alone or in a group. Walking and prayer are great to do together. Meditation is deep prayer. If practiced correctly, it is the highest level of prayer and if done correctly often it will get stronger and deeper and elevate your spiritual soul continually. All people need to meditate <u>in the Christ consciousness</u> to reach higher levels of spiritual being.

How does one meditate correctly? First, as Christ instructed, go into your closet to pray. *But when you pray, go into your room, close the door and pray to your Father, who is unseen. Then your Father, who sees what is done in secret, will reward you.*

(Mathew 6:6)
You must be alone with little around to distract. *What you have said in the dark will be heard in the daylight, and what you have whispered in the ear in the inner rooms will be proclaimed from the roofs.*

(Luke 12:3)
Relaxation is key so take several deep breaths of air and think the Lord's Prayer several times. Jesus said: *In the same way, those of you who do not give up everything you have cannot be my disciples.*

(Luke 14:33)
This means to go deep into your soul omitting all physical life. I do not believe it means to sell all your earthly positions. After all Jesus had "stuff." He had clothes, shoes, a walking stick. Do not fall into the trap that some want others to believe by taking individual Bible passages literally. Giving up everything is to commit everything in your existence to the purpose of being. That is, to commit your total mind and spirit to the purpose of spiritual improvement for yourself and all those around you. There is NO physical existence here.

Next, ask God for the strength, kindness, mercy, humility, and knowledge of the Christ spirit to come into your soul. Don't just think it or believe it, <u>you must know it.</u> This is the "warm ups" to deep Christian meditation. The whole idea is to think of nothing but "Christ like" thoughts in the beginning of your meditation. With practice you learn to think of nothing, and I mean nothing, to reach a state of being where God can reach to you. Do not try meditation without the Christ spirit. This could leave an opening for evil to get into your thoughts. Meditate correctly and often, your spiritual maturity will be elevated continually. Can we as humans reach the Christ level? Christ said we could.

(John 14:12)
Very truly I tell you, whoever believes in me will do the works I have been doing, and they will do even greater things than these, because I am going to the Father.

Maybe that was an invitation or a challenge. I am not sure which but I know God wants us to try. Our goal is to make our soul, our spirit, grow stronger and higher in the levels of the God spirit just as Jesus, the teacher, proclaimed. *Therefore, confess your sins to each other and pray for each other so that you may be healed. The prayer of a righteous person is powerful and effective.*

(James: 5:16)
When Jesus was on Earth the term meditation would not have been understood. Combine these words with Christ teaching of how we will do the same wondrous works that He did. Strong words but backed up by all Christ teachings.

The length of time for meditation is not as important as the quality of the time dedicated. Being in your closet, focused and listening to what God has to say to you at this time is vital. Frequency of meditations is important. Daily meditation and continual prayer are best. Continual prayer? Yes, it is possible and very effective. Remember, prayer is in the mind and the human mind can multi-task. If all actions and thoughts are done with part of the mind in Godly prayer only good will be the results or outcome. These good results may not be today or even tomorrow but they will be.

(Hebrews 6:12)
We do not want you to become lazy, but to imitate those who through faith and patience inherit what has been promised.

Prayer is important to our physical beings and spiritual development. We have all heard this most of our lives since little children going to bed and saying prayers with our parents. Then attending Church and following the established religious teachings and praying in groups. All good endeavors and very valuable to our existence in this universe …. But: <u>not enough</u> for growth. Where is the closet that the Bible teaches us about? Reciting prayers alone, although good, will not raise our spirit development. Just being alone is not in the closet of the soul. All physical thoughts must be eliminated and only deep spiritual meditative communication with God.

TRUTH FOUR

Religion, what is religion? Is it the search for a better understanding of God and His directives? A group of like-minded individuals to meet, socialize, and study a text for an understanding of how to behave? Christ never talked of "having religion," only of having the knowledge of Him and God. Yes, gathering for the study of the Bible is time very well spent.

(Matthew 18:20)
For where two or three gather in my name, there am I with them.

There is no bad religion, no matter how much you may disagree with one. Any group that promotes a God focused study, is good. God is good, He can do only good and wants us to do good always. A group that claims to be God's children and promotes bad is a religion, but not in the God since but only in the physical desires.

What needs to improve is how deep of study does this religious group takes its members. There is no religious organization that can take its members to the level that an individual can accomplish on his or her own self. In this physical plane we control evil. It is our decision to accept evil or deny it. It is our decision to give evil power or make it weak. God controls goodness, we receive the goodness we deserve or request and accept. It is up to the individual soul to develop itself, using and studying the teachings of any and all God study religions. All God oriented organizations are good but none have the answer to all questions. Only our direct communication with God will gain us the correct answers: and only if we seek them. Religions have preached the same message over and over for thousands of years, a great learning tool for the early stages of learning. But, in order to improve (MATURE) we must go to the next level in our spiritual development. Think of yourself as an iceberg, what most are experiencing is the visible tip. Only you can dive deep in the water of the Holy Spirit to learn how big you really are. Make physical life a short-repeated experience in your eternity. We learn by doing repeatedly, improving and growing from the experiences and lessons learned last time. There is so much to learn.

One short 70 to 90-year full lifespan is not near enough time or life experience to get to where Christ and God wish us to elevate ourselves. We must live more than once; this is the only logical explanation. Again, if God can do anything why is this concept so hard for some people to understand and accept? Since this universe is only a God mist, moving from one level to another is an easy procedure for the Supreme Being and us. Your next life could be in this level or another, higher or lower depending on what you learn, apply and retain forever.

Jesus always tells us the truth. His words must be studied deeply and thought of in a manner that He knew a lot more than He explained. This approach will help to open our spirits to levels most fail to perceive. A very simple example of this is in

(Luke 6:46 – 49):
"Why do you call me, 'Lord, Lord,' and do not do what I say? ⁴⁷ As for everyone who comes to me and hears my words and puts them into practice, I will show you what they are like. ⁴⁸ They are like a man building a house, who dug down deep and laid the foundation on rock. When a flood came, the torrent struck that house but could not shake it, because it was well built.

In Chapter 46 I believe Jesus is telling us we will be introduced to The God presence with The Christ spirit at our side if we learn and apply His teachings. It is our responsibility to learn the Christ teachings and live by them. Later in this section Jesus Christ refers to the lessons as a foundation, a start, a strong building block to begin our spiritual lives. Of course, the foundation is the most important part of any building. Without the correct foundation any structure will fall. Jesus explains very plainly that it is His teachings are what we need to build ourselves. And there have been many others though out history that have taught the same messages.

The most important message of this truth is to <u>think</u>. No matter who is speaking or writing, or what the subject matter, we must always think about it. If the subject matter is important and the answer is not obvious (like 2+2=4) then prayer and meditation is needed. Taking the time necessary is important also. Do not hurry to any conclusion. Do not make a sudden mental commitment or physical contract until sure. Always be open to new and advanced topics. Consider any idea that seems a possible and logical theory. If, after much study and prayerful meditation, the thought does not seem right or logical in the God since, then do not adhere to it. But, it is in the mind so make it a learning tool for future growth. Even un-adhered to theory's are a building block for comparisons for development. We must have the maturity to discern right from wrong. Stay away from the illogical and strive toward the logical.

Remember, nothing is black or white. Everything is shades of an incalculable number of colors. The only known: God Is. Until our spirit reaches the highest level this is the only known. Yes, think about the words written here. Consider, pray, meditate and develop yourself. Take nothing presented by human at face value into your soul.

TRUTH FIVE

Praying: Why do we pray? Why is there so many different religions and yet all people pray to a Superior Presence? Some people forget to pray for a while and others refuse to until a need arises, but everyone does. Why? Because: There is a God and we all believe it. Few know that God exist, but all believe it. Humans are made in His likeness so how is it possible to de-align ourselves from Him? Sometimes a people will push the knowledge of God aside, but it is always there. A very few people will even deny the existence of a Supreme Being. But, without God we do not exist and everyone realizes this, sooner or later. This is His universe not ours.

We are here in this element for a reason not by an evolutionary accidental development. The reason for our existence is to become as Christ like as possible. Jesus prayed, Buda prayed, Mohammad prayed, all to worship God. And I would like to believe they meditated often also. Do you need to jump around, waving arms in the air to pray? I don't think so! Actually, I question if this action is prayer at all. I think it is more of a "show and tell" the world how religions you are. Do you need to lead a solemn, lonesome life? To live a life with little outside interaction of the rest of the world will lack much understanding of nature (God). NO, these lifestyles and prayer actions will not do harm to your spiritual life but surely will not help in your study of God's will or find great favor with God's plan for spiritual growth or.

Remember always, <u>anything</u> to excess is wrong. Too much water is harmful, too much air is bad for the indigestion. I repeat, anything to excess is wrong. Too much organized religion will affect your spiritual growth in a negative way. Any types of worship can be done to excess and that is not right. Too much prayer/meditation without a active life is not conductive to an improved spiritual elevation. A thoughtful variety is more productive to a prayerfully studious life experience and learning process.

Go back to the before mentioned action of waving your arms around in the air. This is a religiously taught method of worship and is very low on the spiritual evolutionary scale. Yelling out: "thank you Lord, thank you Lord" is an avenue for someone who does not have anything else to say or do. Nowhere is it written that Christ acted like this in any form or fashion. So whose idea was it to start something like this as a method of worship? There is so much more to prayer and thank you is only an elementary beginning. In itself there is nothing wrong or spiritually harmful to this form of worship but it will not be received deeply by God. Living every day in the "Christ consciousness" is the entire message from Jesus, so that is all the thanks God wants or desires from us. To live as Christ taught is the ultimate goal. WWJD

Speaking loudly "thank you" while looking up, waving arms in the air, speaking unknown babble in a group of peers, does little to really express your gratitude or feelings or worship to Jesus or God. It is all just for "show and tell". Does it hurt your spiritual self, probably not, but it does hold you back and makes you dependent on the organization to which you belong. Do not rely on this to be your total expression of worship to God. What is the logic of these actions? Would you really think God wants to hear such noise? Does this really help in your study to elevate your soul to a higher level? Going to your place of worship on Sunday or Saturday is always a good experience. God is in all of life and all of time. Is God really in the up direction? No, he is inside each of us, so look for God inside you, not up. Go into your closet to pray even while in the religious buildings. Meditate always and alone whenever possible. We must live our Church at all times. Words and ideals that are easier to say than to be done. This is one of the trials and studies that God has daily presented to us.

TRUTH SIX

Belief in God is not enough. You must KNOW IN GOD and KNOW GOD. This is not just a word game. This is the most important message of all. If you know God you have the power, compassion and resources of His Son. These resources can be put to use as explained in

(John 14:12)
Very truly I tell you, whoever believes in me will do the works I have been doing, and they will do even greater things than these, because I am going to the Father.

I believe Jesus was talking about all persons, of any faith, so long as they follow the Christ Consciousness teachings.

A good illustration of KNOWING is to think of yourself standing in the center of a room with people standing behind you. You see a chair brought into the room and taken directly behind you but not touching your legs. You even hear the chair legs hit the floor. Do you have the nerve to sit down without looking? You have faith that the chair is still there but do you know for sure. Has someone stepped up and moved the chair. Will you fall to the floor or will you sit comfortably in the chair? You have faith that the chair is still there but until you touch it and are supported by the chair. Only then will you KNOW the chair is there.

This little exercise is only to show that sitting in the chair, being supported and feeling the security of the chair is the goal. Knowing it is there for you, is much better and surer than just believing it is still behind you. Faith is great in being sure what God will do in support for us as He has always promised and done. But we should know Gods existence by touch and feel and being supported by Him. How does one touch and feel God? Remember what the Bible says, God is inside all of us. Deep, prayerful, devoted meditation, the devotion that lets God come to us and touch and feel our spiritual selves.

Ask most Church or Synagogue worshipers about God and one of the first comments is that they believe in Him and His commitment to us. I think this is a very good start to our religious devotion. But now the Churches and Synagogues need to step it up and progress their followers to a deeper spiritual existence. They are teaching and we are following Christ teachings the same as 2000 years ago. When Christ walked the earth there was little education and little understanding of anything except survival. Today we are smarter, wiser, and understand more about what is around us. I know God planned this time of 2000 years for human development so we can truly find and grow in our spiritual selves. This age of the physical development is the truest and toughest test of all. We have all this modern technology and tools but can we still take the time and effort to improve ourselves spiritually? Or do we just concentrate on and elevate the importance of our physical stuff.

KNOW IN GOD and KNOW GOD …..Yes, I know: *Jesus said, "Believe in God".* (Mark 11:22). But consider this: a person would have to believe in God before he can KNOW GOD. Remember the Bible was written long ago for the understanding and education of the first Christians. Well, it is time for all of us to grow up. It is time for all believers to be elevated to KNOWERS.

TRUTH SEVEN

The Second Coming of Christ will not happen as most are imagining. He did not come the first time as everyone thought he would. So why should we think He would come the second time as Christians are being taught? Two thousand years ago all indications were that the Savior would come as a king, an earthly king to save the people from all their ills and repression. It did not happen that way. Now all teachings and predictions are that Christ will suddenly appear "from the sky to be known to all men."

(Revelation 1:7)
Watch! He will come in the clouds. Everyone will see him. Those who stuck a spear in him will also see him. All the tribes on earth will cry when they see him. That is the way it will be. Yes, it will!

Think about it, have we again put a human aspect to the living God? Jesus will not slowly descend out of the clouds and make a smooth touch down on earth. For one thing, the earth is round and it will be dark on half. These words are for an audience of people that do not know this and only know the world around them.

Go beyond, think deeper, why would Christ come from the sky? I think by His teaching and history of Christ and God's (Nature's) plan will tell us Christ will appear to all people internally. Like a mass baptism to all mankind at one instant moment. This will be an Earth changing experience. Life as we know it today will no longer exist. Those that have spiritually elevated enough and live, or have lived, in Christ's consciousness will be accepted into a higher order of Gods heaven. Remember there is Seven "houses" of heaven and it is determined by us and our various lives which level we deserve. Heaven has "Streets of Gold". This has been repeated so much but is stupid to teach. Why would God's house need anything to do with gold or precious jewels? Again, the phrase is used to paint a picture of a beautiful, beyond words, beyond any place every seen before. But, if not explained this way many of the populist will start to see it this primitive vision and never understand the true meaning. Yes, Heaven is a beautiful and wondrous existence. It is not a neighborhood place with streets. No one knows what Heaven really looks like and if anyone gives you a description of Heaven .... They are wrong.

Is the Second Coming of Christ heaven on earth (the thousand years of peace) or is it the Armageddon, too leave this planet for a better existence? There have been and will be many divisive discussions and writings on this issue. This really is a question of little importance for our existence at this time. It is fine to have an opinion as to which is going to happen but there is no correct answer. No one knows and God wants it that way. God has a plan we are not privy to and it will be done as He intends. We must strive to pass the daily test and learn from our experiences for the elevation of our souls.

God knows that we humans must have a mortar, a teacher to see and emulate. Jesus was sent to teach humans how to behave and develop as God desires for us. We are not to follow teachings of other men or women. From the beginning of time, God knew we would need the Christ teachings and that Jesus would come and this was prophesized throughout the Bible. We are human and He is God. Nature is logical and predicable and always correct. Humans have free will and with decision making powers but we are also predicable. God created us so He knows how we will react to each situation presented in a large overall scheme. Many people will not accept Christ on His second coming. It is written that those who have succumb to the evil side of self will not accept Christ as the son of God, just as most did not the first time. I am sure that many "Christians" will not know the Christ presence when He appears again.

The Christ Sprit, first and second coming, is universal across most Christian religious sects. Any religion that teaches a Supreme love and respect for fellow humans and all of nature have the Christ Spirit in it. Any group that controls the minds of the members with a message to worship only the leader's words and rules, obeying only their commands do not have His Spirit. And the members will parish someday. We are responsible for our own wellbeing and everlasting soul. We make our own decisions to follow good truth or misguiding words. We must think prayerfully at all times and about all teachings.

The second coming of the Christ Consciousness will be to help lead us to the next level of God's spirit. And we can go, but not until we are educated and elevated and prepared. We, each of us, are in control of our own soul's future. None of us know all the correct answers to God's plan, mind or universe. I know the answers are inside each of us and we must continually strive to find them.

May God's presence be in your every thought.
May you always be a blessing to God.

Amen:

THE AUTHOR: RUSS SIMMONS

Growing up in a family that was not Church religious ordinated but very spiritual in thinking and living is a blessing and nuisance. Your family does things and goes places that most others would think was "weird". And you, as a young person, are advised not to discuss these events with friends or relatives because they will not understand and would think it too far out of the norm. After all, this was the late 1950's to middle 1960's and the middle-class world was not yet open to innovative and free will thinking.

Events like this: Our immediate family, some extended family and a few family friends would meet at our house once a week for in-depth spiritual study. I was 8 to 16 years old and was required to attend. This is a lot to ask of a child, especially in the summer, I would rather be outside playing with my neighborhood friends. More conflicting, I could not discuss the happenings with anyone. My father would lead these deep meditative studies. All sessions were in a Christ centered study. He once told me that when he was a young man it became apparent of an unusual spiritual gift and a desire to understand more. Very few knew of this and he kept it very private. My father died when I was 17 and the studies ended with his death.

As a family we made several trips to spiritual advancement seminars with group study, lectures and exercises. Here, even at a young age, I was attending classes of concentrated learning of God and man's relationship with God. Some of these were taught by nationally known leaders of this kind of thinking. Also, were lessons in communication with God through deep personal meditation. The instruction always had a Christian underlying message and emphasis. These workshops were very valuable to me on many levels and I also learned we were not the only people with these beliefs and intensity. At the time I went and did all this because of my age and I had no choice. My parents were being good stewards and teachers of their two sons.

After my father's death I continued the spiritual life I had been taught, still keeping my thoughts very personal and private. At 19 I married and started attending Church and really loved the bible study accomplished here. But still, I must keep the non-accepted Christian thoughts and actions to myself. This is OK because I was accustomed to living this way. After all, there is nothing wrong with standard Christian Church teachings. I feel my three children did observe and benefit from my parenting life-teaching and actions that I instructed towards them daily. And the Church experience was invaluable to their growth and development.

Sometime in the year 2000 while on business trips and being alone in hotels for several days I would be in deep meditation frequently and lengthy. While deep within, I began having thoughts of just sentences and short ideas. Sometimes one sentence other times several. Afterward I would write these down and later concentrate prayerfully on the meanings. Occasionally the sentences would fit together, but not often. This continued for about 4 years, then I began to get serious and writing the sentences in a literary form. For many years the process was just an occasional thought and little work, but did not feel an overly strong need to pursue. For a couple of years, I did very little writing but always continued my constant meditative prayerful life. Then in 2010 I could not pray or meditate without this manuscript being thrust into my thoughts. I began reading my own words, praying, meditating and working to rewrite the correct understanding and message. It all seemed to fall into place.

A lifetime of spiritual training and living has brought me to this place where we meet.

GOD IS
HUMANS ARE

THE UNIVERSE
IS NOT

www.ingramcontent.com/pod-product-compliance
Lightning Source LLC
Chambersburg PA
CBHW072039080526
44578CB00007B/535